YEARS LATER

YEARS LATER

poems
by Gregory Djanikian

CARNEGIE MELLON UNIVERSITY PRESS
PITTSBURGH 2000

ACKNOWLEDGMENTS

Grateful acknowledgment is made to the editors of the following magazines in which some of these poems first appeared:

American Poetry Review (Philly Edition): "Crazy Day"; *The American Scholar*: "Apartment House at Evening"; *Ararat*: "The Engagement," "After the Revolution"; *The Chelsea Review*: "At Midnight Or So," "Phone Call from Arizona"; *The Cortland Review*: "Break Up," "Fable," "You Just Don't Get It," "Waiting For Her Again," "At the End of the Day," "Years Later," "Neither Here Nor There," "The Man Who Was Always Sad"; *Critical Quarterly*: "Something Unusual," "Over Lunch"; *CrossConnect*: "An Episode," "At the Edge of Something," "Brief Romance"; *Georgia Review*: "A Quarrel of Pairs"; *Iowa Review*: "The Trip"; *Painted Bride Quarterly*: "A Gift," "Voyeur"; *Poetry*: "Absences," "The Physics of Traveling Away"; *Poetry International*: "Lac de Nom Perdu," "Lost Love"; *Poetry Northwest*: "Almost Enough," "In the Hospital Room"; *Shenandoah*: "Artist's Return"

My thanks to the Corporation of Yaddo for two residencies during which some of these poems were written. Thanks also to Stephen Dunn and Mark Halliday for their suggestions, and to my wife Alysa for her keen eye and support.

Publication of this book is supported by a grant from the Pennsylvania Council on the Arts.

Library of Congress Catalog Card Number 98-71944
ISBN 0-88748-316-X
ISBN 0-88748-301-1 Pbk.

CONTENTS

FOR ALYSA

All companionship can consist only
in the strengthening of two neigh-
boring solitudes. . . . for when a
person abandons himself, he is no
longer anything, and when two
people both give themselves up in
order to come close to each other,
there is no longer any ground
beneath them and their being
together is a continual falling.
— *Rilke*

Hold tight.
— *Fats Waller*

I

Something Unusual

When it was clear that their marriage
could not continue, when the accusations
had led to punishments—silences, illicit calls, closed doors—
and would not be commuted, when they decided
they could no longer apologize for who they were
or what they had become,
                                        on that day
the furnace backed up, "exploded" they thought,
the black soot rushing out of all the vents
into every room and crevice.

It was like something unusual
falling from the sky, the fine
dark coating over all the surfaces.

At first, they tried to blame it on each other,
which one had not replaced the filter,
which one had noticed the tell-tale signs
of trouble and done nothing.

But soon they thought
why shouldn't it happen, let the house
go to ruin as well, the charred smell
already in the folds of things.

They were standing in the dining room,
she was thinking of the stranger she wanted to become,
he, of the light receding through his many windows.

By chance, she wrote her name with her finger
on the table-top, and liked its declaration so much
after all she felt she had given into
that she wanted to write it on anything she could find,
vases, candlesticks, chairs,
                                        and of course
whether as a joke or not, he began doing

the same in the bedroom, the music box, the lamp, mine, mine
he was suddenly telling himself with such fervor

and when they had appropriated for themselves
everything they could, exhausting each other,
they stood absently and without speaking

in a kind of emptiness
each of them had needed to touch
which had avoided them for so long.

Good Neighbors

After we had chased away
the intruder
who had beaten up
our neighbor next door

and the police
had come too late
and the ambulance
had carted her away

we began thinking
of guns under the pillow
the large knives
we wanted to carry
like secrets why not
we felt soft
easily punctured

we made sure
the cellar was locked
the back door double-bolted
we looked for someone
at the window
someone cutting glass
or the phone lines
even trampling our garden
for mischief

let him come we said
let him suffer like us
what the world
has in store bullet
to the soft eye
the thinnest wire
against the groin

and as for the merciful in us
it was wearing a torturer's face
("pliers," we said,
"blow torches,")
what wouldn't we use
against the smallest
infraction

we wanted to speak
all night in this way
without shame or
explanation we wanted
to say "Like this,

we do it like this"
all the fine hairs
of the skin rising
at our least word

and by the time
we were finished
we didn't know
how far we had gone
or where we had lost
our own voices

we couldn't bear
to touch each other
so much tenderness
would it take now
so much undoing
of what we had said
what it seemed
we had always
been capable of saying

Court Sense

They are playing tennis,
and neither is speaking to the other,
the muscles of their faces
tense enough to hurt.

You can tell she's a strong player,
punishing him with angled
cross-courts, then down the line,
and all she wants from him
is to retrieve, retrieve,
so she can keep drilling it.

It's an agreement, a game
with high stakes, who leads,
who follows, who might be told
to pack or asked to stay.

She's grunting with each stroke,
thigh muscle and calf flaring
through backhand or volley,
the ball spinning madly at him.

You wonder what leads to such
requitals, maybe a bad match
from the beginning, maybe
something more tacit,
suspicions, words misspoken.

Now she's yelling out the score
as she fires overheads toward his body,
love-thirty! love-forty! and it could go on
for hours with nothing but love
between them, love-game, love-set,

or until love finally walks
off the court having given enough,
or too much, or taken everything
it needed to, changing the rules.

Lac de Nom Perdu

The lake is calm, it is night,
the stars are cold and clear

and a man and a woman
are floating in a rowboat

in the middle of the lake
talking now in low whispers

so that no one may enter the space
of their talking or their being

where they are
on the cool dark water

their hushed cries skimming
toward the shore like so many translucent wings

and their transitory kisses
fluttering about finger or breast

and the beaded water
falling off their oarblades

like stars, like prisms
of happiness falling

from a long way off
and with hardly a sound.

The Trip

For several months, he had been
untangling himself from her,
uncomfortable about what kept lingering,
the caresses that sometimes went too far now,
the flirtation that had no place at their table.

They were driving back from a week-end stay
in a city she had always wanted to see,
and he was thinking of the river which wound
through its heart, remembered his feeling
that the future was a far off place,
everyone else heading for it,
everyone waving goodbye.

She asked him suddenly
whether he had *ever* loved her, a question
which took him by surprise,
brought him back to her
where he was used to being.

"Yes" he could have said, "of course,"
the old comfortableness setting in,
but he had been led now to the edge of something,
maybe a declaration which was different from any
he had made before, something riskier
and with the notion of change in it.
"I don't know," he said,
"I can't tell, maybe not."

He saw her face tighten,
half wanted to stop the car, kiss her hard—
this is what I want, he imagined saying, this!—
half wanted to let it ride,
a turmoil inside him making him
stupid and flushed.

He let the moment pass, then for miles,
the grey silent landscape between them,
until there was no going back
with retractions, no undoing her hurt

or the way he had to think of himself now,
as a man with another man inside him
he would soon have to bargain with.

Over Lunch

You feel a strangeness
being with her again, you feel

as if you're thrown *back when*
though you don't quite know

how to behave, whether as you were,
or are, all the old mannerisms

coming back to you, the way
you said *lovely* with three syllables

the way you cocked your head
to listen to her deeply

as you are doing now
while she retrieves old friends

for you, revives occasions
that have lingered like faint incense

and now that she's asking you
whether you've been happy

you can't exactly tell if
she might mean happy in the life

you've lived with someone else,
or maybe happy to have lived it without her

and who could answer such a question
anyway without sounding

inexcusably small in spite
of all you might say,

and suddenly the lentil soup
the waiter has put before you

becomes the most indispensable
part of your life, the croutons bobbing

like small buoys of salvation,
and if only you could float the lightest

of words to her across the table,
if you could say, "Look at the light

changing outside the window,"
or mention the pomegranate seeds

shining translucently
on the fruit cart, or this thick

taste of soup on your tongue now,
this surprise from nowhere

come to visit, requiring
no fanfare, no explanation.

Break Up

It's 1 a.m. at the Golden Grill
and he's looking down at his bourbon
as though he might stick his nose in it,
what the hell, before he gets to the bottom.

From the dark booth in the corner
someone's yelling, "Where have I put my love?"
and that sounds right to him, this sense
of having misplaced, having lost
the location of: if only he could think back,
gesture by gesture, word by word.

Lorrine and the True Sensations
are about to sing "Barrelin' Down to Your Heart"
and he's grateful for something loud and raucous
to keep him together, push
against him on all sides: along the bar,
everyone turning around, giving
his loneliness to Lorrine, all he's got.

If his wife walked in just now
from wherever she was—Idaho, Wyoming?—
he'd do something extravagant, take
half his clothes off, sing *Sweet Wilderness of You*
and dedicate it to the one he loves.

He's been quiet and still so long
he wants to cause a riot, something physical,
maybe meanness sitting on his stool for a change
and having a drink with everybody.

It could go on all night, this feeling
that he's missed something along the way,
something now the couple getting up to dance
might have, all hands with each other,
all thigh-muscle and crotch, tight with the music.

And when he walks out of anyplace now,
he'll know if it's for the last time:
he's seen that walk,
and the door it passes through.

Love turning away, love running out:
he'll be here till morning thinking about it.

Artist's Return

By the way, she says,
I thought I was going to die

coming back from where
I was painting you know

the dirt road through the stand
of birches there out of nowhere

a green pick-up veering
toward me and by instinct

or luck I swerved to the edge
of the woods a miracle

I didn't collide with trunk
or branch (the delicate

paper bark just beyond
the hood) and then a whitish

thin head of hair in the cab
passing by and a hand

waving as if to say
I'm awake now sorry I'm ok

and my life thrown out
and sprawling before me

for a few seconds
before my eye retrieved it

and then the whole way back
the sky cerulean blue

and the cumulus clouds
wind-driven and voluptuous

and me almost forgetting
to tell you because, she says,

my painting by the river
(you should see the speckled

iridescence of mica!) went so easily
and with such indirection.

Decorum

His days are mired in obligation,
a bed of impatiens he ought to weed again,
a lawn neatly edge, his life an exemplum
of too many *no thank you*'s,
so many *I can't*'s.

In his voice, the irritation of someone
who knows he's not dangerous, unlikely
to offend even the smallest animal.

If excess were to visit for a while,
he'd make it paint his house
aquamarine, he'd make love
with all the windows open,
he'd be frank without apology
or say *fuck* in a way
which could be sexy and hard to resist.

So much of the time spent
balancing one number with another
till it's correct, percentages, checkbooks,
and in his heart, a chemistry
which sometimes tips him over.

He'd like to get a new car,
red and sporty, maybe steal it even—
how about the one down the street,
he'll take the woman too,
and who knows more about sparks
than someone about to strike a match?

Fuck the impatiens, he thinks,
needing a drink downtown,
suddenly pleased with himself.

And when he turns the key in his ignition,
he doesn't sense how loud he's gunning

his engine, or care in which direction
he should be pointing now,
or how soon he ought to be going.

A Quarrel of Pairs

The hayfield is harrowed:
a million pores are breathing the light in.

The dead willow is down, chainsawn,
its dry twigs scattered like seeds.

In the neighbor's pasture, a shed tilts to one side
like someone who still has a good leg.

Down Asylum Road, there is no asylum
but you can hear the tinkling of glass.

The crab-apple tree, yes, is half leafless,
half covered with birds.

At the edge of the woods, a clear path
toward nothing you could call transparent.

In the evening, loons, loons on the lake.
How easy to say *lake* without implication!

Night settles down with its dark clouds,
each window-light a tip of desire.

Now her *goodbye*s fall to the floor like stones.
What a roundness of words to hold in your hand.

Tulip Magnolia

The magnolia tree in the backyard had died
and they knew they might have to move,
the cold arriving in all the fissures.

They thought of painting the kitchen
something citrusy, or bright,
but it was the color
of magnolia they wanted,
pale pink like the blossom,
grey like the bark.

Once, when they were in bed,
they smelled the scent of lilac outside
and wished to mistake it for magnolia.

They thought of other trees—lindens,
hawthornes—hoping to distract themselves,
but too often, one found the other
looking at any wall as if it were a window.

How many seasons, real
or imagined, had the blossoms opened
on the day of their anniversary?

Now when they made love
each touch had a rumor
of absence to it.

And on the morning one of them
found the other asleep under the dry branches,
it was understood they would leave,
so impossible was it now

to look at themselves without nostalgia,
or to be apart from one another
without the sense, suddenly,
of someone watching.

Almost Enough

He wants something extraordinary,
a heron feather floating to his hand,
or the Pleiades, all seven sisters,
flaring above his house.

He wants the nearby pasture cleared
of old box springs, all the tractor parts,
he wants his bad neighbor
to fall to his knees, confessing
his love for the Yukon, say,
or the tip of the Australian desert.

He wants people to have
as many suitcases as they need.

But a hundred oboes for his room.
Starfire lilies scenting his every morning.
And what about someone saying *syrup* in just
the syrupy way he could get used to?

Maybe the wind in his dream
will die down long enough
so he can hear what the leaves
have been whispering
all these years.

And what if he could touch everything
just beyond the edge of his life,
the fox deep in the woods,
and the woods deeper within the fox?

If he could move the river now,
five degrees to the left so the sun
could glint perfectly into his parlor,

if he could invert the clouds

so the scalloped edges
would graze along his roof.

It's three in the afternoon
and he can hear the cows in the upper field
lowing to come home, he can
hear the bad neighbor's bad dog
barking again on its tether,

and soon, he'll be hearing nothing else—
just the noise of things
needing to make noise,

like this crow cawing at him
from a pine branch, and the dog again,
and his own surprising voice
answering back.

Seeing

She was trying to see
what he was pointing out,
the Big Dipper, a ladle, he said,
a spoon, a cup with a handle.

But she was feeling the immensity
of sky, grains of wheat
spilled on a dark table.

No, no, he said, focusing harder
for her, his arm brushing her cheek,
look at the four stars
of the bowl, it's simple,
it's like a cave, like a bowl.

She thought she saw a locomotive,
maybe an elephant, something like
a cannon firing sparks.

His hands were on her shoulders now,
turning her this way and that,
tilting her head just right.

Maybe she saw something, a skullcap
with a tassel, or maybe a balloon, or a kite
embroidered with gold stitching,
it's a child's face, she said, it's a hand
opening like a flower. . . .

A dipper, he said, it's a dipper,
why can't you see it?

But she was going on wildly now
seeing whatever it pleased her to see,
torches, coral reefs, magnificent oaks,

and as he turned to walk away
having done all he thought
he could do for her

she was just moving
to that part of the sky
where already an arrow was shooting
through the heart of things,
and a swan waiting to fly into her life
whether she could see it or not.

Meteor

It was the Great Bear
I had come out to watch
and the stars of the Corona,
Cygnus the swan
poised at the zenith
in the almost-autumn night,

but it was a meteor
arcing slowly toward Perseus
and another falling
against the fixed template
of constellations and a third
burning as long and bright

that won me over, meteors
blazing yellow-white,
unhinged as if like stars
from the sky, *there*
and *there*.

It was this after-image of light
I took home and tried to revive
through my telling of it

but it was the sense of falling
that returned me to the open field
under Jupiter and its moons
sublimely in their orbits,

it was these heavenly others
I waited for which could not stand,
unleashed and plunging down
in a sudden bountiful light, falling
and flaring as if to say
we were all beautiful once.

Absences

This is for the cat who is missing,
to bring her back to the fold,

who had been slinking nightly toward
field mice and mole, quietly, weightlessly,

with suppleness of forepaw and haunch
until shrieking its cat-shriek twice

in the cool, echoing air where pasture
runs to brook, it disappeared.

And this is for coyote too,
prowling along the upper ridge,

for fox stalking by hummock and culvert,
for great horned owl by stream bank,

each waiting for the odor, the leaf rustle,
of cat, cat, cat, to enter their lives.

And this, too, is for the child
left inconsolable at the bedroom window,

for the father returning field-weary and empty-handed,
and the mother whose touch is no comfort,

and the restless mind
that keeps traveling out

to where tooth might have sunk into muscle
or great wings borne away the likeness of cat.

This is for the dream of mouth or grip
and for those caught in the sudden truth of them,

and this is for the others who are left behind
at the edge of a field, or in doorway,

hearing only the sound of that dream,
hearing it without certitude, without end.

II

Fable

A man was singing from a scaffolding,
How can I begin to bear her love?

The traffic below was slowing down,
women were smiling, thinking of themselves
in the song, all the men were trying
to come up with a song of their own.

The police were putting up cordons,
fire brigades were hooking up their ladders.

When she longs for me,
I feel a migration in my blood,
he was singing, his hands on his heart.

Such a magnetic disturbance
on all the radar screens, helicopters
circling above him, skywriters
advertising *Eau d'Amour.*

Then the explosion of applause
when he had finished, some people yelling *More!*
and others writing down all the words.

By the time he had climbed down,
people had been singing the song
through the streets, pleased
to hear their own voices.

Already, tourists had begun converging
on the city in large groups, each one
with a dictionary and the newest maps.

Later, no one knew where the song had come from.
Some said the sky, others remembered a book.

You Just Don't Get It

I will lavish on you nasturtium
and rose, she said, I will bare
my throat for your kisses.

Her words were a powerful elixir,
all my aches were trembling to depart.

I will stand, she said, in the window
of light, waiting for the birds
to wreathe their songs about me.

This was a real feat, I thought,
a phenomenological rarity.

I will make you a linen suit of my love,
I will sew it with laughter
and a hundred difficult questions.

Another new emperor, I imagined,
but the question part was intriguing.

Tell me your true name, she said,
the stars will embroider your initials,
the zodiac will spin with anticipation.

Speaking of anticipation, I was feeling
a little edgy, & what had happened to the throat thing?

My bed is a bower of blisses;
under the cool sheets, the waterfall
of my deepest desires will sound.

Bingo! I thought, in my lady's
chamber, no mistaking the signs.

Let my heart call forth
a republic of joy, it will sing

above a choir of the darkest clouds.

This was taking a bad turn, this jaunt
. *toward the airy (eerie?) heavens.*

Let the doors of my heart
open only to the touch of no touch,
love's mysterious fluency.

Touch of no touch, what did she think
I was, Mr. Invisible? & that door business. . . .

My lover is a cockleshell
I wear by my heart, my lover
is the absence inside it as well.

Listen, I told her, earth's
the right place, etc. . .so maybe another time.

Summer is a wind in my blood,
and fall glories about my heart,
then winter's frost is love's sting.

She had some good things to say I remember,
but the chemistry, sheesh, you know what I mean?

A Gift

A man was polishing his shoes
in front of his cottage
with turpentine and bleach.
The leather was changing
color, flaking off.

You're ruining your shoes,
his wife said unhappily from the kitchen,
look at the mishap you've created.

People were stopping by,
offering her their condolences.

The priest said a prayer over him,
the police chief wondered
if some foul play were involved,
the marriage broker, shaking his head,
looked at his long list of names.

But the man kept to his shoes
all afternoon, smiling at his wife,
humming a tune they had learned together.

In the evening, when they went to town,
everyone snickered behind his back,
pointing at his shoes
as he shuffled along like a crab.

But his wife, they said, had never
looked as beautiful in her ruffled dress,
the way she walked on his arm
in front of all the shop windows
and restaurants, the way she clicked
down the street among a hundred eyes
with such style now, such inexplicable ease.

Waiting for Her Again

She has been *late* so many times
the word by itself
has lost its meaning,
the undertone of accusation
you have always counted on.

When you say she is *late*
you might as well say
"She is of medium height,"
that lack of resonance.

Now you are standing on a corner
looking at your watch and thinking
of gradations of lateness,
very late, incalculably late,
which, far from giving you a sense
of sanctimony, are making you nervous.

She clicks toward you then
in her red shoes,
red, you think, the color
of blood, of choler.

All right, you say, tell me of the upheavals,
the circus wagons upended, the lemurs
overruning your house, maybe all the buttons
of your skirts snipped off.

"I must be late," she says,
without shame or sense of history.

If there were pigs on a leash
grunting across the street, or a man
in a carrot suit singing "O My Papa,"
you could point to them, you could say,
"That's just what it is, madness, madness!"

But there's nothing really
except her smile taking you easily in
and her hand brushing back her hair
as if to say "C'mon," and steering you again
toward that emporium of wishes
just beyond every next corner,

where you'll be late in arriving
as often as you wish.

Voyeur

He looks at her from his window,
a woman sitting on the grass
reading a book.

Sometimes she looks up
as though she knows she's being
watched, how she shakes her hair
to free it of something.

He feels oddly dangerous,
one impropriety permitting him
perhaps another and where
would it end, his life
suddenly unraveled?

He wishes he were a character
in the book she's reading,
maybe cooking eggs in Altoona
or discovering his true name
at the Last Dance Motel,
but always, his attention fixed
on her merest gesture, an insistent *I*
staring up at her from every page.

To watch under cover of being watched:
he could be so openly intentful that no one
would think to be astonished!

Now she rubs her calf
and he feels it on his skin,
she turns the page and a draft
wafts across his arm.

He wants her to be happy, wants her
to find his roses on page 74,

and further on, along the terrace
overlooking the Adriatic,
to hear him say *we are never alone.*

Now she rises to stretch her legs,
and just as he feels himself unwind,
she shuts the book, closing
the many doors of his body as well,
a dark sky suddenly lowering
on all he could have done for her,
all they might have been.

An Episode

"Betrayed, I am betrayed!" he says,
wobbling in a drizzle of rain
with his coat unbuttoned and no hat on.

We find him in the middle of the street,
his shoes in a puddle,
the soaked city all about him.

"She's left for good, driven off
with my life!" he cries out
to the tallest buildings as we try
to maneuver around him.

Maybe she's miles away
in a breezy convertible,
maybe she's managed to go as far
as the other side of town—

but what a spectacle he is among us now
with his arms upraised and his mouth
stuck open to the sky like a pullet's.

"The end of the world," he shouts
flinging off his coat and shirt,
and water dripping from his head
like a circlet of tears.

Won't someone steer him gently home
before the whitecoats come
with winches and manacles and straps
to keep our peace, and keep him quiet?

We press closer together, one body
smugly against the other,
pull up our collars against the cold and wet:
Not our fault, we think, moving on,
not our life, or what our life will come to.

We walk a long time hearing him
behind us, his voice around the corner,
or finding us now from over the rooftops,
and just as we feel him bearing down
too quickly and turn to look

we see there's no one there,
no one at all following us home,
and no one putting the key to our lock,
and entering, and knowing
where everything is.

At Midnight Or So

The train whistles past my window,
wheel squinching against rail,
metal on metal. That sound.

A song on the radio: The Crash Test Dummies
singing something about sad love
across the breakfast table—and I wonder
how we keep surviving the crumple of the heart.

Someone now is heading home,
someone is leaning into the stiff wind and ice
and holding on to the invisible rope
of his life while a bough breaks
or a tire skids into error.

And my children: walking to school tomorrow,
sledding down the sheer slopes through
the bountiful trees, how can I keep track?

In my dream there's a road to a river
I haven't reached: an empty chair
by the riverbank, a book's pages
riffling among blue irises,
and from far away, the thick bramble
of my imagination trying to make sense.

Now a sharp cry: the cat at the door,
or the door swinging on tight hinges.
Or what I always have to think:
an unfamiliar palm pushing it open,
the moment verging in a hushed
silence toward melodrama.

Now the train: gone by forever.
A light is flickering on and off.

Everywhere I turn, something
seems to ask without thought
or malice, What do you
make of this? And of this?

Tourists of Dolor

The visas were obtained too easily,
the getting there, instantaneous: *goodbye, goodbye.*
And always during the wrong season.

*

So many restaurants to choose from
but never more than the one dish, and later,
the feeling of never having eaten.

*

In the great library of a hundred walls,
only the book with blue letters,
thick, and with all the names.

*

A guide was pointing at nothing in particular
under the archway of sighs,
and everyone was taking pictures of each other.

*

Near the public fountains, a garden bed
had been dug and turned over.
Nobody was certain of what to do now.

*

A man looking lost, holding
a colorful balloon: *Help me,* he was saying
to the policemen with all the pins.

*

No one had been in love
for a long time: even the rain
had forgotten to fall indiscreetly.

*

The deportations had been
scheduled for years, and everyone
was going to be next.

At The End of the Day

You are walking home
while the city shimmers
in the hot summery distance—

(*Today, today,* says the train
pulling away from the station)—

and the cracks in the sidewalk
are like the turns of a story
you've been following
thinking they might include you.

A bottle of wine, a splash
of roses are peeking out of your satchel
like bulletins for a new life
maybe just around the corner.

Three tulips by themselves
are stunning the afternoon
with their yellow open hearts;

and the cat's blue eye: a glittering
among the many periwinkles.

And someone calling out from a window,
"Hello, hello, hello," maybe
to you, maybe to no one
you can see at the edge of evening.

The porch steps rise toward
some dénouement, the green door
waits to turn on its hinges—
each breath is poised, you think,
for this moment:

your hand on the knob, the latch
clicking open: then darkness
rushing out and taking you in,

and everything returning
easily to itself again

as if your passing through
were only rumor or recollection,
as if you had arrived a long time ago.

Years Later

There's a tree he remembers
in whose branches
are many rooms
hidden by the leaves.

If he finds it, which may be soon,
he might have to call from below
for someone to set down a ladder.

He thinks he knows who lives there,
all his old lovers, even his wife
he hasn't seen for a while,
one happy family.

How long has he been gone?
How far into the desert could he have walked
in his bare feet and without a hat?

Now in the distance he sees
a shimmering of green, he hears
the sound of water in the leaves.

"Sweethearts," he coos,
putting his hand on the trunk.

But the tree is shaking violently.
All around him, small birds
are falling out of it,
singing off key.

Neither Here Nor There

It is where you think you've been heading,
though you're never quite certain
if you've already arrived.

But here you are at the marketplace,
asking directions to the town hall—
you'd like to update your records,
your passport photo, marital status—
though you're not sure what declarations
are required now, and don't you detect
a quiet civility in everyone?

You think you hear the sound of water
though you're not sure
if it's only a memory of it:
were all the fountains dismantled years ago,
or just hours before you came?

And the dust swirling around your feet,
the newsstands with their empty bins:
how easy to be the stranger
without expectation.

The sun has been at 2 o'clock
all afternoon, the one cloud in the sky
small, inauspicious.

Now in the town square,
a clatter of hammers:
you see the gallows being built,
the noose expertly tied.

And someone in a hood
walking beside you now,
either executioner,
or thief about to be hanged,
leading, or being led.

The Man Who Was Always Sad

After he had ordered
the breakfast sausages
on the first day of his honeymoon,
his wife had excused herself,
inexplicably struck
by how odd and unendurable
her life had become.

*

His dog with double vision:
it would run to meet him at the gate,
though always it seemed to prefer
his second, illusive self.

*

Bewilderment
hung over him
like a cloud.
And when he spoke,
so many flowers
about to fall
off their stems.

*

His sadness was an artifact,
people always coming up
and wanting to touch it,
though, once, when he wrote
a compendium of his life,
it put him in too much
good humor.

*

At the piano bar:
all the diminished chords

sliding to his side of the table,
all the peanut shells
collecting around his shoes.

*

When he smiled, everyone
knew the machinery involved,
so many ropes to adjust,
so many gears and pulleys.

*

Once, on the third day of a fast,
he began seeing visions,
wolves lapping at the throat
of an angel, a woman in flames
calling to him from a lake,
and not even the desire
to be the throat, to be the flame.

*

How many words had the grass
taught him as a child
which he had now forgotten!

*

The wind kept
rattling the door
of his house,
but he was startled
only by the sound
of another door
closing quietly
somewhere else.

III

The Engagement

It is Alexandria in 1939,
before the war, before the invasion guns
have overrun the desert, and the lights
in all the windows have gone out.

The Mediterranean is turquoise and ethereal
and the wind from the sea at Stanley Bay
is winding now around my mother
who stands on the beach in her Sunday dress,
half-dreaming, and her heart flung open.

In the cabana behind her, a radio
is crackling with news from the north,
her uncles are shouting across a backgammon table,
there are bathers-to-be in colorful trunks,
and children squealing in the oncoming tide,

but she's not attentive to any of it
because walking the curve of the beach toward her
there is my father in his white linen suit,
all of twenty-two and smiling,
a creased new handkerchief in his front pocket
and white carnations in his hand.

How wonderfully out of place they seem,
her frilly dress among the beach towels,
his thin-soled shoes filling up with sand!

Such happiness! though soon enough
the war will linger, and the unforgiving years unwind
from around desire and a heart that flutters.

But to have them now so young and without guile:
my mother calling out my father's name,
my father waving, and quickening his steps,
the carnations nodding their heads a thousand times *yes*.

After the Revolution
Alexandria, 1953

We were standing at Montaza along the beach
the year after Farouk had abdicated
and the iron gates to his summer palace
had opened for all of us and the sunlight
was sparkling off the water like coral.

It was evening: the old fishermen
had begun casting into the surf
and already one of them had caught something large,
we could see the rod bending against the weight.

By the breakwater, a man was cupping
his mouth with his hands and calling out
"Jean-Paul, Jean-Paul," toward the sea
where the cross-currents were heaviest,

and there was a ship passing further out
beyond the impounded royal yachts,
steaming toward Beirut or the Aegean
and blowing its long, dolorous horn.

Soon it would be getting dark
and there would be a line of cars traveling
the Corniche back into the heart of the city,
a thousand headlights illuminating
the night, like Pharos, for a safe passage.

Someone was running now
on the white sand with his arms raised
and shouting, "Egypt for the Egyptians!"
and another was putting a green kite up
like a flag above the cheering crowd
and there was a sense of things
picking up speed, converging.

Further away on the palace lawn,
a company of soldiers were drilling with rifles
and bayonets, we could hear drums in a rhythm,
and sometimes the clattering of steel
as though the war which was going to come
had already arrived, the deportations
and imprisonments begun
and the Suez, wrenched
loose from Europe, were on fire.

We were standing near each other now—
my father, Berjoui, M. Goganian—
feeling the sea air against our faces,
the rumor of its salt on our skin.

By one of the white cabanas,
my grandmother was shucking sea urchins,
serving them up to us like miniature
mines on a salver, the orange meat
juicy and still alive in the black half-shells,

my mother, my grandfather half smiling,
and Mme. Yazgy holding my hand, trying
to close the circle of family and friends
as we began eating, the sharp taste
of the sea suddenly filling our mouths,
and the sun behind us, floating like a cauldron eye
over the water, huge and unblinking.

Histories
Lebanon, 1969

While Mme. Fernan and her lover
were kissing on the darkest side
of the balcony of the Hotel Najar

two men on a lit terrace in Baabdat
were rolling dice and slapping
their backgammon tiles
on the playing board

and down a mountain road from Bhamdoun
several donkeys were braying
under their baskets of figs

and the monastery bell in Is'haya
was ringing the canonical hour

and in Beirut at the Club Mediterrané
Nino Ferrer was singing "A Hundred Good Nights"
while the ocean liners in the harbor
were still glittering like stars

and the pointed moon
had not yet crested over Souh-el-Gharb

where Mme. Fernan and her lover
were slowly undressing,
startled now and then
by their small explosions

of happiness, exhalations
of surprise in the arcing night
before all the other nights to come.

Apartment House At Evening

Something about a hundred windows
lit up like a ship's upper decks, something

about the weed trees
tossing like water below

and the cumulus steam
from the boiler stacks billowing away

and something, too, about a woman
taking off her heels and leaning

dreamily on the balcony railing
as if there's an ocean about her

and something about the laundry
strung up between apartments

like flags signalling the future
and about the samba now

wafting in the cool breeze
and moonlight falling from everywhere

and Nevrig dancing on the rooftop with Aram
and the city blazing with lights

like a harbor about to be left behind
with its customs house and identity cards,

the lines untied, the deep
horizonless night rolling in.

At the Edge of Something

Do you remember the café
by the sea, the boats bobbing up
and down at their moorings
like so many assents?

And the men at the other tables
trying hard not to look at you
and failing, failing.

So long ago! So much dazzling water
and sunlight, and the words between us.

Old love, what a silence now for years:
where is the news, the rumor of you,
the book in which your name is emblazoned?

And my younger life in yours:
to be able to hear a trace of me still
in the way you used to whisper.

Now I am thinking of the photograph
that could have been taken of us:
a young man smiling under the brim of a hat,
the young woman in a loose dress
unfurling about her body like a sail.

Then the one boat
beyond all the others,
moving laterally in the distance—
ours, you said, *ours*—gleaming,
cutting deep in the water.

The Physics of Traveling Away

What a tedium of days without you.
And everyone looking at me as if I were lost,
a man sighing for no reason
except that his breath has been taken away.

Tell me you've arrived without notice,
that the cafés have not been overwhelmed by you
and the men in the public squares
have all shrugged without feeling.

Outside my window, lovers passing by
and their slow walk causing in me what riots.

At the corner fruit stand, mangoes,
Damascan figs sometimes, the sudden
wild taste of you where you might be.

And the few letters I tear open
with their faint odor of what has already happened:
I want the now, now, now of your news!

Such punishment, this staying in one place,
and the road to somewhere else
always a block away, another city over.

And that last night: all the traffic lights
to the airport turning green,
speeding you on and making you
already how much younger.

Even the way I look at your photograph—
the stranger you are becoming!—
as if the slightest disturbances of memory
could add on months, years.

In the Hospital Room

He has been talking to her mostly about food,
maybe to distract her, or trick her body
back into health, or maybe because
he has always loved talking about it
and she has loved hearing him.

He is whispering to her now
of their anniversary dinner two years ago,
the grilled squab on a bed of mango slices,
the nine-spiced dumpling which surprised her
with its hundred corners.

There is a whirring of machines in the next bay,
bubbles are rising in one of many tubes.

He is remembering for her the *Côte-d'Or* in 1957,
the *potage royal* embroidered with dill,
the truffles en cassoulette, he is
describing the Medoc in which simmered
the sweetbreads of two angus calves.

Each time he reconstructs any one of five sauces
he brings his hand to his heart
as on his wedding day
as if a great veil had suddenly lifted.

But how much uncertainty has accumulated here
like invisible clouds around everyone!
And the doctor with his charts and percentages
and the intercom blaring, "Number 4, please, number 4."

Maybe tomorrow the lucky skies
will have opened up for them
and ten-thousand raindrops fallen for joy.

Maybe it will go on like this for most of the evening:
she listening intently, nodding her head yes
to the memory of sea urchin and yellowfin,
hummingbird soup and chickory leaf

while nurses whisk in and out
and the guerneys in the corridor
glide by like boats

and his low voice wrapping around her now
with *vol-au-vent au poisson, calamari fritti,*
and the checkered tablecloths lightly rising

in the breeze, the white linen napkins,
such delicate violets painted on each plate.

Lost Love

Someone is walking up and down the street
crying "My lost love, my lost love!"
without shame or consolation.

On a day for columbine and lilac,
for hearing leaves sigh in the wind,
so many spring groves are in the making,
so many different orchestras tuning up.

My lost love: a refrain which scatters like bird shot.
How many of us have gone to the window
feeling the words pierce our morning.

In my room, gardenias once:
your body floating over me, my skin
rearranging like water under your touch
and your urgent heart, that loveliest extravagance.

Poor man outside, whose sadness
idles like a hearse in front of all our doors.
And some of us climbing in without meaning to!

In the way you held your neck,
Kiss me you would say: then the world releasing
its perfumes from the garden of gardens,
and the body speaking in tongues again

wildly without reason,
without any hope for reason.

Brief Romance

Your dog in my apartment: you've brought him
with you, and now that we're in bed, body to body,
I can't help looking at his soulful looking back,
pressing us for all our pleasure to unwind.

Such a collection of strangers between us:
dogs, ex-lovers, lovers-to-be who are already
rumors about my heart—where is there leisure
or roominess in all my thinking?

Soon you'll be flying to North Carolina,
or Utah, somewhere suddenly extraordinary
because it's where you'll be touching down:
dozens of new encounters then, spectacular
events about to occur without me.

"Be with me," you say, and I'm all breath
and bedroom lips, my day running out
with how many sweet goodbyes,
how many *baby*s strung together.

On the slate roof, a steady rain.
Against the floor, your dog tapping his tail:

So many clocks this afternoon.
Such little time making so much noise.

Driving Toward the Border

It was in Nebraska where the Platte
weaved its many strands through farmland
and prairie that we began fighting again,
hearing our bad voices—fidelity, desire,
who had enough, or too much.

We had been talking of the stark, elegant landscapes
farther west where we were headed
and the sun bleaching the bones
of cattle and mule deer and javelina:
a cow skull for our doorway, you said,
horns to hang above our bed.

Now there was bad traffic between us,
a heaviness which wouldn't go away,
the expansive roads we had been taking
across piedmont and badlands
going on too long now,
how would we ever survive them.

In Laramie, a shaft of moonlight
hit the floor of our motel room
like a sliver of ice and you slipped
under it, taking on its color
and said, if anyone touched you now,
you might shatter like the light
you had become, like the silence
we had been living with for so long.

The days were magnetic:
we hadn't made love for a week
through Wyoming, Utah, most of Arizona,
the desert landscape that took our breath away
and always, this desire to touch everything.

And when we finally hit Douglas,
we walked into the only hotel in town

with its slow ceiling fans and cut-glass lamps,
and the long dark bar some ranchers
were leaning easily against
and talking about line fencing and sacaton
along the steep arroyos—

a few Mexicans from the border ranches
were laughing over their beer at the corner table,
and through the windows, just further south
beyond the chain link and barbed wire,
we could see Agua Prieta and the desert
stretching away to somewhere else,

and how little it would take, it seemed,
for us to start again, to cross over
to that other side without baggage or passport,
strangers, suddenly, travelling light
and beginning to speak to each other
in a language we couldn't remember having learned
and in words which were never ours.

Phone Call from Arizona

My wife tells me she's going to sleep
on a flat-bed truck tonight
in the middle of the desert.

I'm thinking of coyotes,
I'm asking her now about the mountain lions,
the mule deer with their nuzzling mouths.

She says it's the space she likes,
the nowhere that goes on for miles,
and besides, she's packed a .44,
the rattlers won't even come to bother.

"Tarantulas," I say, "what about them,"
and already there's a twang to her,
a couple of beers maybe,
a loosening of her body
pitching her voice just right.

I'd rather be there with her, smelling
the southwest in her hair, maybe running
my hand up along her northern 40
under a rhinestone-studded sky

but all I'm imagining now is tooth and muzzle,
I'm thinking diamondback and Gilas—
"Relax," she says, "let me tell you
about the cholla blooming like fire, the birds
a lipstick red, and the broadest sky"—

and I'm hearing cattle in a stampede,
bulls suddenly gone crazy with love,
"Scorpions," I'm telling her as she
sends me a kiss through the wire,
"fierce horses," I say just before

I hear the phone click
like a tongue, like a spur,
or a gun barrel turning.

Just Because

We were in the foothills
of the Sierras, as though in a movie,
as though we had planned it that way,

riding bareback in the late afternoon
with a breeze behind us
and our horses gentle and without guile,

and even the six vultures
around the dead calf we passed
edged quietly away unfurling their wings

and the sidewinder under the rocks
shifted slightly into the shade
and the sound of the hooves through the grass

was like water all around us,
the smell of horses and sagebrush
as I had always imagined

and if someone had hollered
buffalo over the rise
I wouldn't have been surprised

because the clouds were drifting
on a long trail west
and the rivers of my desire

could have been flowing anywhere
we were because we were
in that kind of day, miles

from nowhere and in open
country because the wind
had been taking us easily

in any direction and our horses
were side-stepping mound and burrow
because even our words

among scorpion and thorn
had been falling all day
in just the right places.

Crazy Day

A flower truck has stopped
by the curb: everyone's rushing to it,
people losing their hats, buying flowers.

And the whistles policemen keep blowing:
too many lovers behind the wheel,
so much swerving to keep hold of!

From a third-floor balcony window
a woman is leaning out,
her nightgown is slipping open
but she doesn't mind, she doesn't mind,
the wind is curling around her
like the softest boa.

Everywhere the neighborhood is unloosening
and love is having its mysterious revolution.

And we're in it too:
"Undress me," you whisper, turning us
into such thieves of the morning,
the cats outside yowling to get in,
the telephone ringing,
Not here, not here, not here!

Even if for a day, a few hours,
love turning the tables on us:
wanting to be wherever we are,
bumping into us from all directions.

Anniversary Poem

How many times have I slighted you
with sharp retorts, kindnesses taken for granted,
selfishness refitting me in its expensive suit
in front of the finest mirrors.

The man who thinks he can do
without love: a man feasting
too long at his own table.

Forgive me, I have written often
on a hundred sheets of paper
folding them carefully on our bed
like so many flowers about to slowly open.

And those quick, passionate claims
on our younger lives: how different they were,
the heart unreeling upwards like a kite,
and all too easily the cut string, goodbye.

Now the years are collecting
like all the pages of a good long letter
we have been writing to each other—
the crossed-out words, the wayward sentences
included—anniversary after anniversary.

And here we are again, our morning opening out
around cinnamon and coffee on a silver tray,
the tenderest wet morsels of pineapple, plum,
and mouth against mouth.

Such an unhurried time together,
this late afternoon, late evening:
the windows open, the trees at ease in the wind,
the luxurious heart forgivable, and forgiving.

Resonances

You want a face as open
as the moon's, your smile
revealing to her
even the darkness behind it.

When she asks you what you feel,
you want to say *love* as easily
as others might say nothing,
though you'd like a certain
elusiveness to remain, a slight
hesitation as before each breath.

You'd like her to read
between the lines
of your palm, though how lovely
if she found there a language
she's never spoken.

Now as you touch her wrist
part of you unravels,
but isn't it in the geography
of desire, this needing
to lose one's way?

And when you say her name,
never does it seem enough,
as if several letters were missing,
and the one at the heart—
unpronounceable.